Strange Nests

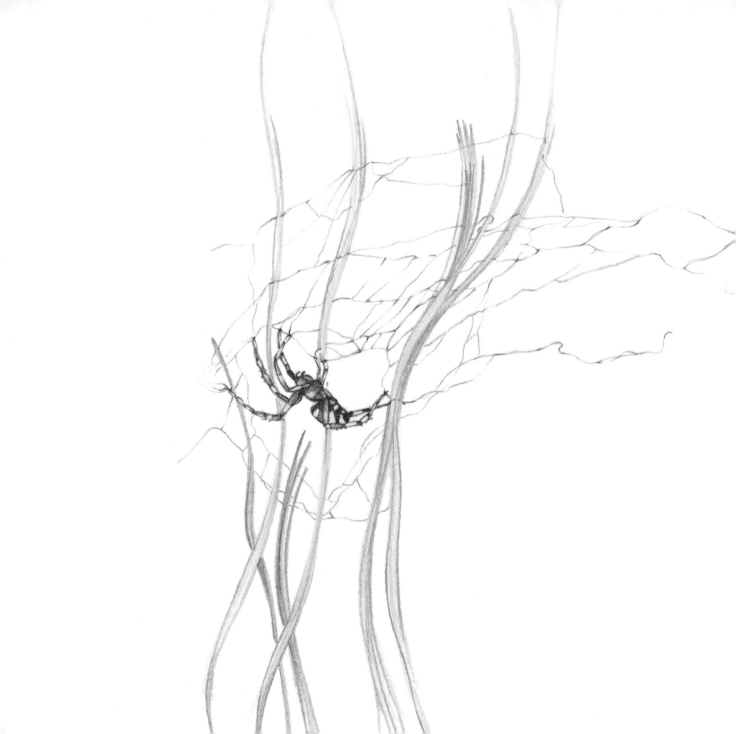

Strange Nests

Ann Shepard Stevens

Illustrations by
Jennifer Owings Dewey

THE MILLBROOK PRESS
BROOKFIELD, CONNECTICUT

Contents

Foreword

It's not easy to find a bird's nest, and it's not supposed to be. Birds are born knowing how to build a strong nest in a safe place. That place could be in the sand, on top of the highest tree, or on its own little island in the water. Wherever it is, the eggs that are laid are usually a color or pattern that helps keep them — and the nest — a secret.

Although they begin with instinct, nest-building skills may improve with experience. Nests are usually sturdy enough to hold the eggs that are laid, and strong, to protect the hatchlings as long as they need protection. Many birds will reuse old nests year after year, adding more materials if needed.

Most birds use plant materials for their nests, like grasses, twigs, straw, roots, leaves, bark, and flower heads. They know that early morning is the best time to build, when dead grasses and other materials are still moist and flexible from the dew. Then the birds line their nests with soft, warm materials, like feathers, down, fur, and even tent caterpillar or spiderweb silk. This lining provides insulation and shelter for eggs and hatchlings in all kinds of weather.

Some birds make their nests in a few hours, while others may take days or weeks. Birds work very hard flying back and forth to their nest sites. Sometimes they make hundreds of trips, carrying twigs and other nesting materials a little at a time with their beaks or feet.

If their nesting material is in short supply, birds are surprisingly adaptive. One pair of wood thrushes built their nest almost entirely of paper napkins and tissue. A female song sparrow used only short pieces of wire. Pigeons have nested on nails, coots on plastic bags, storks on old clothes, and ravens on barbed wire.

Birds' nests have always been a mystery to me. I have looked for nests in all seasons, read and listened to stories about nests, and now I have written a book about nests, both strange and stranger. I hope you will enjoy reading *Strange Nests* as much as I have loved writing it.

Ann Stevens

American Robins

A robin's nest is one of the best built of all songbirds. The female builds a deep, cup-shaped nest of grasses and weed stalks, which she weaves together. Mud is also an essential ingredient, strengthening the nest as it hardens.

Sometimes robins will travel as much as a quarter of a mile to find it. If none is available, they make it by dipping their feet in water and standing in dirt. The birds scoop the mud up in their beaks, and the female molds it into the nest with the curve of her body.

In the early 1900s a robin built a very unusual nest in a tree in Boston. She wove in two red satin ribbons, which read "New York N.E.A. at Boston, 1903." Near the rim was a piece of white lace through which she had threaded two white chicken feathers and a dollar bill. She decorated the rest of the nest with brown and yellow string, a piece of blue silk, the hem of a handkerchief, and some white satin ribbon.

Another pair of robins in San Francisco built a nest on the overhead running wire of a streetcar. The female robin stood up every time the trolley wheel ran by a few inches below her nest, then settled back on her eggs after the car had passed.

Swallows

Barn swallows build their nests under ledges or the eaves of buildings—barns being one of their favorite sites. Often an old nest is repaired and reused. Besides grasses, horsehair, and feathers, they use mud, and lots of it. Like the robin, the barn swallow will travel up to a half mile away for more than a thousand mouthfuls of mud.

The tree swallow builds its nest in tree holes or man-made boxes. The nest is made of dried grasses, pieces of straw, pine needles, and white feathers. Nobody knows why swallows prefer white to other colors, but they use these feathers to line their nests, tucking them in so that the curled tips curve over the eggs like a roof. The birds have been known to pluck feathers from live chickens and ducks, and will fight each other for feathers that are floating in the wind. One hundred and forty-seven herring gull feathers were found in a swallow's nest on Cape Cod.

A pair of tree swallows once tucked their nest into a small opening on a ferryboat that traveled back and forth across the St. Lawrence River between Ogdensburg, New York, and Prescott, Canada. They had gathered nesting material from both sides of the river.

Wrens

House wrens like to nest in the cavity of a tree or stump, but because these are getting harder to find, they will nest almost anywhere. Besides using the deserted nests of other birds, they have built in the paper nests of hornets, cow skulls, cubbyholes of desks, fishing creels left outside, rusty tin cans, mailboxes, iron pipes, teapots, old boots or hats, pockets of scarecrows, and pants hanging from a clothesline.

A pair of Carolina wrens found a slightly open window in a house and built a nest inside, in the torn upholstery of a sofa. The owners sealed off the room, and the wrens successfully raised their family. Another pair built their nest on a farm tractor in daily use around a field in Georgia.

Ospreys

Ospreys build their nests in treetops and other high places. If storms haven't destroyed the big sloppy nests, ospreys will reuse an old nest, adding more sticks, seaweed, bones, driftwood, and cornstalks, as well as rope, fishnets, broomsticks, toy boats, old shoes, straw hats, dolls, welcome mats, and other trash from marshes and beaches. One man found a towel, several shirts, and his garden rake in a nest.

Ospreys usually nest near water, on living or dead trees, utility poles, stadium lights, duck blinds, fishing shacks, cranes, and on man-made platforms attached to poles.

Like wrens, ospreys have also nested on moving objects. A pair of ospreys in New Hampshire built a nest on an old windmill. When the wind blew and the rudder turned, the female sitting on her nest swung around and around as if she were on a bird-sized Ferris wheel.

13

House Sparrows

House sparrows find many nesting sites around houses—under the eaves, on porch rafters, behind shutters, and in holes in the walls. They will fill a birdhouse in a day with grasses, weeds, hair, cotton, string, and chicken feathers. Equally adapted to city living, they nest in the hollow crossbeams of street signs and lights, as well as in ivy growing on apartment buildings.

Sometimes house sparrows nest in the outer walls of eagle, hawk, and osprey nests. The presence of these large birds protects the nest from snakes or raccoons, and the sparrows also pick up scraps of leftover food brought for the baby birds of prey.

In one season a pair of house sparrows built a nest in North Carolina that contained 1,282 items—mostly grasses and strips of grapevine bark, but also a piece of a letter with the typed words "difficult struggle." The birds added candy wrappers, cigarette filters, cellophane, Kleenex, cotton, thread, twine, Band-Aids, and twenty-eight bluejay, cardinal, and catbird feathers.

Nests play an important part in the life of house sparrows. Not only do they build them to protect their eggs and babies, but they use them at other times of the year for resting during the day and roosting at night.

14

Bald Eagles

The largest nests in North America are built and added to year after year by bald eagles. They carry very large sticks and branches in their beaks or talons and build in the forks of giant trees. The finished nest, called an *aerie* (ar-ree), can weigh more than a family-sized car. An aerie in Ohio that was known to be occupied for thirty-five years was estimated to weigh about 4,000 pounds (1,816 kilograms) when it crashed to the ground.

Eagles may raid garbage dumps for their nests. Children's toys, lightbulbs, shoes, underwear, bleach bottles, magazines, and comics from newspapers have all been found in abandoned aeries.

One man found an aerie at the top of a construction crane in Florida. He called the state highway department, and they continued their roadwork with a new crane, leaving the one with the aerie alone until the eaglets hatched and flew off.

Tufted Titmice

In the eastern part of the country, tufted titmice begin nest building in late April. They will nest in birdhouses, but prefer abandoned woodpecker or squirrel holes in trees.

The bottom of their cupped nest is lined with strips of bark, dried leaves, mosses, and dry grasses, and then padded with hair, fur, and bits of string and cloth. Titmice seem to be especially fond of shredded snake's skin if they can find it. Some people wonder if this is because the skins are both soft and strong, or if the birds somehow feel it will scare off predators.

Titmice have been observed boldly swooping down and plucking hair from live woodchucks, rabbits, mice, squirrels, opossums, dogs, and cattle. One titmouse walked back and forth on the back of a treed cat plucking its hair. Even humans sitting quietly near a nest site have had hair pulled from their heads and beards.

The female titmouse continues to bring material to the nest during egg laying, and uses it to cover her eggs when she leaves to feed.

Ruby-throated Hummingbirds

The ruby-throated hummingbird builds one of the smallest nests in the world, as small as half a Ping-Pong ball. The tiny sacklike nest is camouflaged with lichen from trees, so it looks like a bump on a branch.

    The female starts on a limb with a foundation about 1 inch (2.5 centimeters) long of bud scales, the winter covering of flowers and leaves. Then she builds up the sides, decorating the outside with lichens and mosses. She lines the nest with soft down from ferns, milkweed, fireweed, thistles, and young oak leaves. She then uses one of the strongest materials in nature, silk stolen from spiderwebs, to strengthen and bind the nest together. The top of the nest is curved inward like a cup to keep the two eggs, the size of jelly beans, from rolling out.

Baltimore Orioles

High up in a maple tree, a female Baltimore oriole chooses her nest site toward the tip of a long, slender branch. This makes it safe from heavier egg-stealing squirrels or raccoons. She makes a deep pouch by tying grass fibers to supporting twigs and uses hair and grapevine bark to weave a suspended nest, finishing it from the inside out.

Like other birds that live near people, orioles use materials not found in nature. Besides recycling old nests, they have included 75 feet (23 meters) of white string, strands of bright, many-colored yarns, ribbon, strips of cloth, fish line, and plastic tape from a cassette. One pair built their nest almost entirely out of the crinkly cellophane grass found in an Easter basket.

Yellow Warblers

The yellow warbler's nest is one of the most beautiful to see. Securely built in the fork of a tree, it is a compact nest of silver-gray plant fibers, fine grasses, cotton, and shreds of bark, and lined with plant down and silk from caterpillar nests. Most of the nest is finished in two days with small additions for a day or two after that.

Cowbirds, who do not build their own nests, often try to sneak their eggs into a yellow warbler's nest. One study found as many as four out of ten warbler nests had been invaded by cowbirds. Some wise warblers build a second nest over the cowbird egg in the first one. One very hardworking female built a six-story nest until she was sure that her eggs were the only ones she was hatching.

Crows

Crows are one of the most intelligent of all birds. A pair in Bombay, India, built their nest with 25 pounds (11 kilograms) of gold eyeglass frames they had stolen from an open shop window.

Male and female crows build a large basket of sticks, twigs, bark, and vines in the tops of trees 20 to 60 feet (6 to 18 meters) high. They line their nest with shredded bark, plant fibers, mosses, twine, rags, wool, seaweed, grasses, leaves, feathers, fur, and hair. There have been several records of crows building on chimney tops.

Crows also love bright, shiny objects and snatch glittering items like gold wedding bands, thimbles, tinfoil, and colored glass to complete their nests.

27

What You Can Do to Help Nesting Birds

In early spring, you can help birds by supplying nesting boxes and natural nesting materials like pine needles, grasses, straw, small twigs, leaves, mosses, and flowers. Drop them in a pile on the lawn or snag them on the limbs of trees or shrubs. Create a mud bath for robins and swallows by soaking a bare patch of ground.

You can also offer animal hair, short pieces of string, cotton, yarn, dryer lint, wool, and strips of paper and cloth. You might include brightly colored ribbon in hopes of seeing the nest in the winter when the leaves have fallen. Put this material in small wire baskets, open mesh bags, or wooden containers attached to trees. You never know what the birds will take.

It is against federal law to remove a bird's nest, so if you find one, be sure to leave it alone. In the spring, birds will sometimes leave their nests and babies if people get too close, and in winter, birds, mice, and other small animals use the nests for shelter.

Books For Young Readers

Bailey, Jill, and David Burnie. *Birds*. New York: Dorling Kindersley, Inc. 1992.

Burnie, David. *Bird*. Eyewitness Books. New York: Alfred A. Knopf, 1988.

Kress, Stephen W. *Bird Life: A Guide to the Behavior and Biology of Birds*. New York: Golden Press, 1991.

Peterson, Roger Tory. *Peterson First Guide to Birds of North America*. Boston: Houghton Mifflin Company, 1986.

Other Books About Birds

Baicich, Paul J., and Colin J.O. Harrison. *A Guide to the Nests, Eggs, and Nestlings of North American Birds*, 2nd Edition. San Diego, CA: Academic Press, 1997.

Collias, Nicholas E., and Elsie C. Collias. *Nest Building and Bird Behavior*. Princeton, NJ: Princeton University Press, 1984.

Dunning, Joan. *Secrets of the Nest: The Family Life of North American Birds*. Boston: Houghton Mifflin Company, 1994.

Ehrlich, Paul R., David S. Dobkin, and Darryl Wheye. *The Birder's Handbook*. New York: Simon & Schuster, Inc., 1988.

Harrison, Hal H. *A Field Guide to Birds' Nests of the Eastern United States*. Boston: Houghton Mifflin Company, 1975.

Stokes, Donald W. *A Guide to Bird Behavior*, Vol. 1. Boston: Little, Brown and Company, 1979.

Terres, John K. *The Audubon Society Encyclopedia of North American Birds*. New York: Wings Books, 1980.

Terres, John K. *Songbirds in Your Garden*. Chapel Hill, NC: Algonquin Books, 1994.

For Mom and Dad, with love—
I wish you were here to read this.

A.S.

For Tamar

J.O.D.

Published by The Millbrook Press, Inc.
2 Old New Milford Road
Brookfield, CT 06804

Library of Congress Cataloging-in-Publication Data
Stevens, Ann Shepard.
Strange nests / Ann Shepard Stevens ; illustrated by
Jennifer Owings Dewey.
p. cm.
"A Millbrook Press library edition."
Includes bibliographical references.
Summary: Examines the nests and nest-building habits
of eleven birds common to the continental United States,
as well as unusual nests that have been built when
normal nesting materials were in short supply.
ISBN 0-7613-0413-4 (lib. bdg.)
1. Birds—Nests—Juvenile literature. [1. Birds—Nests.]
I. Dewey, Jennifer, ill. II. Title.
QL675.S74 1998
598.156'4—dc2l   98-4582   CIP   AC

99-15953

Date Due

MAR 9 JUN 5			